WAR CHILD

Memories of a
World War II Childhood

WAR CHILD

Memories of a
World War II
Childhood

MAURINE MURCHISON

CF4·K

10 9 8 7 6 5 4 3 2 1
© Copyright 2010 Maurine Murchison
ISBN: 978-1-84550-538-7

Published in 2010
by
Christian Focus Publications,
Geanies House, Fearn, Tain,
Ross-shire, IV20 1TW,
Great Britain

Cover design by Daniel van Straaten
Cover illustration by Fred Apps
Other illustrations by Fred Apps
Printed by MPG Books Ltd. Cornwall

Scripture quotations are taken from the Authorised Version.
These stories appeared orginally as articles in the magazine
The Explorer.

Contents

Sounds Alarming 7

A Tired Old Bear 13

A Family at Prayer 19

A Safe Shelter 25

Completely Clean..33

Porridge in the Press...41

Home and Away..47

A Strong Dutch Tulip..55

Flames in the Fog 61

Crowds for a Coronation 67

My Name is Anne 75

The Hiding Place...81

Who is Maurine Murchison? 90

Psalms for Life 92

What was the Second World War?...................................94

Who was Who in the Second World War?.........................96

Second World War Time Line 100

Second World War Daily Life...102

Sounds Alarming

On a visit back to the city where I was brought up – London, England, I found myself in an old Anderson shelter. These constructions had appeared all over the place during the Second World War as when the bombs fell they provided shelter and protection during the raids.

This shelter was different however. It looked the same inside and out as there was nothing in it but two plain wooden benches standing on an earthen floor. But instead of it being at the back of a London garden it had been rebuilt as part of an exhibition about the London blitz.

The dim light when they shut the door made it very hard to see but that wasn't the worst thing. It wasn't long before the noises started. They would have been frightening to anyone, but for me they were particularly unpleasant. The whole experience brought back disturbing memories of my childhood in London during the Second World War. What I heard were the terrifying noises of an air raid during the blitz. Of course there were no real German bombers overhead but I still felt scared and anxiously waited for the all clear signal to sound.

The most upsetting noise of all was the air raid siren. I remembered that awful sound which had been used to warn Londoners that a wave of bombers was coming. As soon as people heard the siren they had to take shelter without delay. However even though the air raid alarms were very upsetting, they had been life-savers during the war – if you responded to them.

In the made-up shelter I remembered what it had been like to be a small child wakened up from a nice warm bed and shoved, half asleep and protesting, into a red siren suit. This was a kind of zipped up dressing gown.

Once inside the suit my parents would then rush outside into the cold night air to find shelter from the bombs.

There were only a few minutes to spare, made more pressing by having to find the dog who always hid when he heard the noise. Later on in the war things got far worse when the V2 rockets and 'buzz bombs' were used. These would come without warning at any time of day. If one of those was being aimed at your street there was little, if any, opportunity to take shelter.

Alarm signals have been used all through history to alert people of danger to come. The Old Testament tells the history of the fall of Jericho when the Israelites blew rams horns each day as they encircled the city walls.

They were warning Jericho of the judgement that was to come to the city.

How terrified the inhabitants must have been as they watched the Israelite army marching around the city day after day. How frightening to hear the horns blowing and the marching of hundreds of feet!

Only Rahab and her relatives had a secure place to take refuge. Rahab had hidden the Israelite spies from the Jericho soldiers. Because of her loyalty and help she had been given instructions about what to do when the battle commenced. She was told to stay within her house and hang a scarlet thread from the window. This would be a sign to the Israelite soldiers when they came to attack. Rahab's house and anyone within it would be spared. Rahab obeyed the instructions and her household was the only one rescued from the destruction of the city.

The Bible is full of alarms for us today. These don't come as air raid sirens, nor as rams' horn trumpets. These alarms are the words of God himself. They do not alert us to the destruction of a city like London or Jericho but they do warn us of something much more lasting. They warn us of a destruction that will never end.

For example, the writer to the Hebrews alerts us with these words, 'How shall we escape, if we neglect so great salvation?' (Hebrews 2:3).

But it's not all doom and gloom. These words come with a message of hope and absolute security if we do obey them. Even a strong air raid shelter in London would not protect a family if it suffered a direct hit by a bomb. All it could do would be to protect its occupants from falling bricks, broken glass and fire. But God's protection is complete and secure for those who respond. His word urges us to flee to Christ for refuge. The sin that will bring on us eternal destruction can be cancelled and forgiven when we come to Christ for forgiveness. Sheltering under the blood of Christ we are completely safe for time and eternity.

Bible Reading
Read the story of Jericho
in Joshua chapter 6.

A Tired Old Bear

The toy bear was old. Once upon a time he had been fresh and new, golden-haired and plump. But that was many years ago when he was first bought in 1941. So he was now sixty-four years old and all those years of wear and tear had made him look very worn and scruffy. Yet in spite of his looks he remained a very precious bear. He never had another name except 'Teddy Bear' and this is his story.

When I was a little girl I lived for some time in Scotland near the seaside. It was the beginning of World War II and I had come up from London to escape the nightly bombings.

In the country, on the Island of Rasaay, I would be safe and away from the danger. However, during my stay there I took ill with whooping cough. I coughed and coughed all winter and eventually became very ill with pneumonia. In those days there were no antibiotics to deal with the dangerous infection, so I was taken by ambulance to a hospital in Glasgow and settled in a large cot beside a window in the children's ward.

There were no toys in the children's ward apart from a big book called 'My Favourite Book'. Of all the toys in the world the one that I longed for most of all was a teddy bear. However, by the second year of the war it was extremely hard to find toys to buy. There were far more important things to think about. People had to work hard for the 'War Effort'. Families scrimped and saved in order to purchase the essentials like food and clothing.

But my mum wanted to at least try and get her sick little girl what she wanted. She walked the streets, in and out of shop after shop but the answer always was 'No, I'm sorry we don't have a teddy bear!' Almost ready to give up, she tried a little shop underneath a railway bridge.

The shopkeeper hunted in the back and came out with the last toy bear, wrapped in a brown paper bag. He had brown glassy eyes, a nice warm stitched smile and was stuffed with straw. How I loved him! When mum left she tucked him into the cot beside me. When it was time for sleep I hugged him closely and didn't feel so lonely.

Then one night as I lay in my cot I heard a terrifying sound that I had hoped never to hear again. It was the sound of an air raid siren. Suddenly there were footsteps, my cot was covered with a large grey blanket and I was quickly wheeled out into the corridor. This time there weren't any Anderson shelters – instead the children's beds had been pushed into the corridor to protect them from flying glass should a bomb land near by.

Anxious and scared I hugged my bear and longed for my mother to come. I think I might have even prayed that God would send her. Then as I lay in the dark pretending to be asleep I thought I heard a familiar voice. Pulling the grey blanket apart, I peeped between the cot rails and to my joy I saw my mother standing there talking firmly to the nurse.

Even though there had been bombs falling over Glasgow my mum had come to get me, determined to take me home as soon as the 'all clear' had sounded. It was safer in her opinion for me to be back in my own home by the sea than to be in Glasgow on the night of the Clydebank blitz!

It's no wonder that I kept Teddy safely for all those years. He lost most of his hair and nearly all his stuffing. His brown eyes fell out and green buttons were sewn in instead. Knitted dolls' clothes were used to keep his leg and arms from falling off. Yet even though he is so worn out, he is still a VERY SPECIAL BEAR.

Everything we use in this world eventually does wear out, especially if the toy or article is well loved and well used. And these changes don't just happen to things we use and love but also to our bodies as we grow older.

It has happened to me, that little girl in hospital grew up to be a granny and she looks quite different after all those years. Even children grow and change rapidly from year to year. Many children are excited about birthdays and can't grow up quickly enough. But many adults are afraid of change and of growing older. Our society judges people by how they look and what they wear. Many try to improve the way they look or to stop ageing.

The Bible teaches us to have a quite different understanding of what it means to grow older and change. First of all we need to understand that change and decay for boys and girls, men and women are a result of sin. Death came into the world through Adam's sin and change and sickness precede death. However hard we try we can't prevent it happening to every one of us.

Secondly, the Bible teaches us not to look on the outside. The important matter is how each one of us stands in God's sight and God is able to look into our hearts and see what we are really like. We cannot pretend before him. There is a verse that tells us this in the book of 1 Samuel. David had been chosen by God to be the next King of Israel. Samuel was sent by God to David's home to anoint the chosen one. When he arrived he wondered which of Jesse's sons was God's choice for ruler. Samuel himself was impressed by David's older brother and thought he must be the one to become king.

'But the LORD said unto Samuel,"Look not on his countenance, or on the height of his stature; because I have refused him; for the LORD seeth not as man seeth; for man looketh on the outward appearance, but the LORD looketh on the heart"' (1 Samuel 16:7).

Thirdly the Bible tells us the wonderful truth that whatever we may look like, young or old, handsome or ugly, fresh or worn out, if we are Christians, 'though our outward man perish, yet the inward man (or the real person) is renewed day by day' (2 Corinthians 4:16). The Holy Spirit will be working a transformation in us, making us more like Jesus and giving us the real beauty, which God requires. The theological word for this is 'sanctification'.

It is comforting for us to know that even when we are young we need not worry too much about what other children think of our looks and lifestyle.

I haven't thrown out my tattered old bear. Even though he has a bald head and floppy limbs I've treasured him because of what he meant to me as a very sick child. When we look at others it is important not to judge them for how they look but for what they really mean to us. And of course there is something much more important to think about. We need to know if we are acceptable in God's sight through trusting in Christ for forgiveness of sin. Pray daily to become more like Jesus as the years go by.

Bible Reading
Read the story of how David was anointed king of Israel in 1 Samuel 16.

A Family at Prayer

I found an old Bible the other day that my father used to use for our family Bible time or worship. He would use it every day. His finger would stroke the fine rice paper pages. And if you looked closely you could just see the faint pencil marks he had made by some of the verses. Today yellow stains mark the pages where his fingers had leafed through the books of the Bible year after year. It brings a warm feeling of thankfulness to my heart when I see this old Bible. I'm so thankful for a godly upbringing and constant teaching from God's word. But I'm afraid to say that as a child I wasn't always so thankful.

One morning as the Bible was being read I was fidgeting. It was half past eight, time to go off to school and there I was kneeling down as my father prayed on and on. It always seemed as if he was extra long when I was in a hurry and I disliked the embarrassment of still being in the middle of family prayers when my school friends called. Sure enough, the bell rang and I had to wait till the prayer was finished before opening the door.

As soon as my father said 'Amen' I jumped up, gathered my school bag and coat and went out quickly to join my friends. They knew the family pattern and were patiently waiting outside but it still felt a little awkward. None of my friends had Bible reading every morning. It made me feel different and I didn't like that.

Family worship took precedence over everything else. There was no skipping it to dash out to school and it had a very regular pattern. My father took up the family Bible, already well thumb-marked and worn, prayed and read a few verses of a Scottish metrical psalm. My mother and I would then join him in singing this psalm.

On weekdays we would sing from one psalm to the next. We read the Bible in the same way from Genesis to

Revelation. Then the family knelt as my Father prayed to God before he carefully marked where we would begin our Bible reading the next day.

The only day that was different was Sunday, the Lord's day. Every Sunday morning our family would read Mark chapter 16, the story of Christ's resurrection, then in the evening we would read Isaiah chapter 53. The psalm we sung on Sunday was always Psalm 68:18-20, sung to a tune called 'Sheffield'.

Nothing would interrupt the worship time in my family. Whoever was staying in the home or visiting at meal time was expected to join in. If the phone rang during our worship time it went unanswered. If any of my friends called at the door they just had to wait.

As I grew older I would come downstairs after doing my homework, to join in the evening worship before going to bed.

Thankfully over time I grew less impatient and I stopped being embarrassed about our worship time. In fact now I think it is a shame that many families have dropped this practice of gathering together to read God's word and pray. There are many lessons that we can all learn from a faithful pattern of family worship. It may be that your family doesn't read the Bible together but you can make sure that you read it on your own. Apart from it being the right thing to do, there are great advantages in daily Bible reading and prayer.

Firstly, each day is set out in a right context. We are reminded that all we have and all we are come from God the Creator. Whatever worries or interests we may have we can set them before God in prayer and we can commit everything to him. God's word tells us that he is sovereign and in control. We can rest believing that he maintains the world we live in.

Jesus urged his disciples not to worry about what they should eat, drink or wear, but to seek first God's kingdom because their heavenly father knew that they needed those things (Matthew 6: 25-34).

Secondly, we need to learn daily about Christ and examine our relationship to him.

It's so very easy to get so taken up with all the exciting things that are happening at home and at school that we forget about eternal realities and push them aside. But a daily prayer time encourages us to remember we are sinful and to think about our responsibility to respond to the gospel. It is so much better to experience the 'new birth' when we are still young and can give our lives in service to Christ. Ecclesiastes 12:1 reads 'Remember now thy Creator in the days of thy youth, while the evil days come not'.

Thirdly, there are Bible verses, which commend this pattern.

In the Old Testament there were evening and morning prayers in the Tabernacle. Daniel refused to give up his habit of praying three times a day. He knew that it was more important to worship God in this way than to give in to the demands of a foreign king. The New Testament tells us how our Lord Jesus frequently went alone early to pray. If Jesus needed to spend time in prayer how much more do we!

Finally, and perhaps most significantly, by praying regularly we ensure that God is given the most important place in our lives.

We live in a culture where God is mocked. He isn't recognised and respected. To begin and end the day with prayer, be it family or private, ensures that we place the living and true God at the heart of all our days.

So, if you live in a home where the Bible is read daily, don't be embarrassed about it but thank God that this is the example you are being set. Perhaps it will even give you a chance to explain to your friends the comfort of knowing that God is in control and the importance of committing their lives to him through Jesus' sacrifice. And whether your family meets for prayer or not, be sure to read the Bible and pray regularly putting yourself each day into God's loving care.

Bible Reading
Read John 17 which is one of Jesus' prayers.

A Safe Shelter

It was a dark, cold night and nobody could find Scampy. He was in the house somewhere but refused to come when we called for him. My mother knew he was hiding and frightened but we just didn't have the time to search the whole house for the little dog. The air raid siren had sounded and we had to get to shelter quickly. The house was tall on three floors with two long flights of stairs and he could be under a bed or crouching in a dark corner.

We didn't have an Anderson shelter in our garden but there was a public shelter nearby that we used whenever the signal sounded. However, dogs weren't allowed in the public shelters so little Scampy would get locked up in the cellar for safety. He hated this. When the siren sounded our little grey Cairn terrier knew what was about to happen. So he would immediately disappear and the family would rush around the house trying to find him.

But the dog wasn't the only worry for my mother – I caused her more than a little bit of anxiety.

I didn't hide under my bed like the dog did, but I would refuse to even get out of it! Every time the air raid siren sounded my mother would get out my warm red zip-up suit, called a 'siren suit'. It was just the thing to protect me from the bitter cold outside but I hated it. As fast as my mother got it on me I would fight and struggle and pull it off. Half asleep I would then snuggle back into my warm bed in the little attic room at the top of the house.

But our family had only fifteen minutes to get out of the house before the German bombers would be overhead on their way towards the centre of London.

With great effort my mother would shove me in the suit before dragging me down the curly top flight of stairs, down the long straight steps covered in linoleum, towards the front door and out into the cool night air. The public air raid shelter we used was just round the corner in 'Rainbow Street'. A strange name for such a dull and dreary little road! Small terraced homes were closely packed together and most of the folk living there were hard up and some had no jobs to work in.

The shelter was a low brick building at the side of the street, rather like a shed without windows. There was no glass because people could be hurt if a bomb broke the windows. Each shelter held up to fifty sitting on wooden benches often all night long.

That night with the dog safely in the cellar and me wrapped up warmly in the suit my mother and I slept as best we could till the 'all clear' sounded in the morning. There was no sign of Father. He was a doctor and had gone down the road to where a bomb had set a huge paper factory on fire. All night long Mother waited anxiously, wondering how many casualties he was working with and whether many had been killed.

When the wooden doors of the shelter opened in the morning I thought it was still nighttime because the light was so dim outside. However as we made our way into the street we realised that the dim light was a result of the smoke that filled the air. Thousands of tiny pieces of burnt paper floated down from the sky. Along the road we could see the devastation.

Thankfully in the midst of it all we had been kept safe.

The red brick building had been the best protection that my family could find in the early days of the London bombing. Yet that public place of safety was not really very safe. If a bomb had fallen very near it, or worse still, directly onto it, anyone sheltering inside would have been hurt or more probably killed. London was becoming a 'City of Destruction' and the only way to

be safe was to go as far as possible from it. Many, many children did just that.

They were 'evacuated' to the countryside to places where the German bombers were not likely to strike, often far away from their parents for four or five years. Eventually this was what happened to me. Later my parents also left London for the same reason.

Some of you may have read the story of another family who fled from a 'City of Destruction'. It was written well over 300 years ago, is still in print and has been a best seller for many years.

The author was called John Bunyan and he wrote his story while in prison in Bedford. Eventually it was published and the book was called 'The Pilgrim's Progress'.

It is the story of a man called Christian, and later on of his wife, Christiana, and her children. They all left the City of Destruction on a pilgrimage, which took them to the 'Celestial City' or heaven. Though modern children may find the language difficult to understand, Bunyan originally wrote this, his most famous work, to entertain his own children when they came to the jail to visit him.

The story begins with Christian, the pilgrim of the title, under great spiritual stress as he tells his relations how he has read in a book (the Bible) that the city in which they live, 'will be burnt by fire from heaven'.

Of course this fire was not to be started by German bombers, like the London fires, but it was to be the judgement of God on an unbelieving world. Christian was terrified as he understood he was 'condemned to die, and after that to come to judgment'. However, a man called 'Evangelist' told him to 'flee from the wrath

to come' and the rest of the story is an account of how he did just that, lost his burden of sin and eventually, after many adventures, crossed the river of Death and reached the Heavenly city.

Later Christian's wife and family made the same pilgrimage illustrating the joy it is when whole families are united in following Christ.

But 'Pilgrim's Progress' is much more than an exciting adventure story. It is what is called an 'allegory', or a story that has a deeper meaning. We as sinners need to flee from God's wrath and become Christians. We must repent of our sin and trust in the Lord Jesus Christ. We will meet with trials and difficulties but we will also be encouraged and have Christian companionship as we journey to heaven.

My family and I were in great danger during the blitz. We knew that we needed a better shelter and that we had to leave London completely to seek safety elsewhere.

So it is in the spiritual life. We have to turn our backs on our sinful lives and set our faces towards Heaven, seeking to lose our burden of sin at the cross of Christ.

Bible Reading
Read Psalm 91 to find out
how God is our shelter.

Completely Clean

It was Monday morning. That meant it was wash day and a day that promised great fun for me as a little girl. I wasn't old enough for school and so the exciting things depended on which day of the week it was and what was going on at home.

All the family washing was done on a Monday and it mostly happened outside unless it was very wet. In the 1930s there were no automatic washing machines and no chance to do a quick wash every day or so. Instead my mother used a round tub with a sort of spindle stick or paddle in the middle which went back and fore, back and fore. This was where I found my fun!

The tub was on wheels and was dragged out to the back door and into a small yard. There it was filled with steaming hot water by a hosepipe from a gas geyser and tap in the scullery (or utility room as we would call it nowadays). Then two metal boxes were set up on wooden crates and filled with clean cold water. Cathie's mother sorted the dirty clothes into piles, first the whites, next the coloureds and then the really grubby dark things. In went the Sunlight soap flakes and the lighter clothes, the paddle in the middle began to go 'whoosh, whoosh' and the washing began. If I stood up on tiptoe I could watch the clothes swirling around and sniff the lovely soapy smell.

But what I really enjoyed was the warm feel of the suds as they bubbled up on to my face. I would feel really important when I helped to catch the nice clean clothes as they came out of the wringers after the final rinse. Once the clothes had been hung up on the line, I could run in and out of the washing, playing hide and seek and feeling the clean damp material on my skin.

The best fun of all was to be had after all the washing had been done. The ground was all slippery and soapy and I would delight to splash in the rainbow puddles

and kick up waves all down the narrow yard against the brown wooden fence.

However even though it was fun it wasn't as safe as it might have seemed. For one thing, if the lid was off the machine, I could get a sharp electric shock when I touched the tub. For another, it was all too easy to get my fingers caught in the electric rollers which wrung out the washing.

One Monday morning there was almost a disaster. Perhaps my shoes were new and the soles were shiny, perhaps I was just a bit more jumpy than usual but as I splashed around all of a sudden I slipped and fell very badly. I hit my head heavily against a wooden seat and had to be carried into the house and laid down on an old horsehair sofa. There was a deep gash underneath my

hair and the blood kept coming and coming all over my clothes and face.

The cut was so deep that many years later I can still feel the dent that the fall made. I have never forgotten the shock and pain.

Sometimes the washing never got really clean. Living in a city meant that specks of black soot from chimneys were blown on to the clean clothes; not every stain came out completely. Of course the blood stains on my clothes after that accident were almost impossible to remove.

When I visited a church in Holland something I saw there made me remember those Monday mornings spent in the wash tub. A text in English was painted on a cream wall behind the pulpit. It was a verse from Psalm 51; 'Create in me a clean heart'.

But I also thought about the story behind the verse. The Psalm speaks not about the stains and pollution on our clothes or even on our bodies, but about the much deeper marks left by sin on our hearts.

King David of Israel had been stained by serious open sins. When he became convicted of his guilt before God he realised how he could never wash away the dark stains, which lay on his guilty conscience. He turned to God and asked him to give him a new heart, clean and fresh and free from the guilt and pollution of sin.

However young we are, all of us have lives spoilt by the effects of sin. It is just as if we are wearing clothes which have been marked and the stain hasn't come out. Often we can say to ourselves that nobody notices, that it is only a little mark and in any case our clothes are much cleaner than any one else's.

It's only when we are expected to have perfect, unmarked clothes for a special occasion that we become

conscious of the spots and realise that we are not up to the standard. It's a bit like this in the Christian life. God demands perfect cleanliness from sin and nothing else will do. It's not enough to compare ourselves with others, not enough to try to get the stains of sin out by ourselves or to cover them up and ignore them. We need a 'clean heart' and only God can give us this. We need, like King David, to be sorry, to repent of our sin and ask God for the cleansing which comes from trusting in the perfect righteousness of Jesus.

When David was convicted of his sin this led to his understanding of how stained his life was and turned him back to the Lord as he wrote Psalm 51. Perhaps next time you sing this psalm you may think of an 'old fashioned' wash day and how the stains of sin are never completely washed away unless God does it for us.

Bible Reading
Read 2 Samuel 12: 1-14
to find out how David became
convicted of his guilt and sin.

Porridge in the Press

It was half past eleven in the morning and I sat in the kitchen waiting for the dreaded sound. Inside the old wooden kitchen cupboard, or 'press' as it was often called in Scotland, was a bowl that had been kept aside to be shown as evidence. It held a portion of cold, solid porridge, covered with a little milk and no sugar. This had been my breakfast which once again I had been unable to eat. Four hours ago it had come steaming hot from the stove but even then I could only be persuaded to taste a mouthful.

Why didn't I eat it? Perhaps it was because I was missing my parents. I was only four years old and I had been evacuated from London for my own safety, evacuated all the way up to the north of Scotland. However, I think the reason that I didn't eat my breakfast was simply that the porridge made me feel sick, but whatever the problem no threats or encouragements could make me obey the strict instructions of Granny. 'She has to eat her porridge!'

Granny was worried that her granddaughter was refusing food which could keep her strong. On no account was the porridge to be given to the dog, or thrown to the hens. It was to be kept so that she could see for herself exactly how much I had eaten that morning.

And now the moment of truth had come. It was breakfast time. I knew Granny would come into the kitchen and ask Mary, the home help, to take out the plate from the 'press'. She would then decide for herself whether I was still disobedient.

At last I heard the dreaded sounds at the top of the schoolhouse stairs. Thump, thump went the footsteps and then the walking stick banged on each step.

I panicked and rushed out of the front door round to the back of the school. Inside the children were busy in

the two big class rooms, sitting at their wooden desks and scratching away with their slate pencils on their slate boards. But I cared for none of this.

'Where, oh where could I hide from Granny?'

I had to decide what to do quickly. Where could I go? The playground was wide open. I didn't dare run away over to the trees by the shore and so quickly I pressed myself into a corner between two walls knowing full well that if Granny were to come round the corner, she would easily find me.

Minutes later I heard the sound of footsteps on the pebbles, two steps and the thump of a stick, two steps and the thump of a stick. And suddenly Granny was in view, a frightening figure, clad all in black and waving her walking stick.

I have never forgotten that moment of discovery and the fear I felt. But I can't remember if I ate up the porridge or not.

I'm pretty sure that Granny took me back to the kitchen, faced me with the bowlful of neglected porridge and scolded me for disobedience but the stick was never used to punish.

A few weeks later I left the lovely island to go back to my parents. I never saw my Granny again.

For many years I would remember my Granny as a threatening figure in black, waving a stick. But then one day I found some of her letters and I realised how much Granny had missed me and loved me.

While looking at some old photos I began to see that the smiling person who had taken me in and looked after me for one summer in wartime, was a very warm Christian who had cared for me dearly. And even the story of the porridge showed how much she cared. She was worried that I would fall sick if I didn't eat enough and she was determined to make sure that I kept fit and well.

Right at the beginning of time, the first man Adam and the first woman Eve were disobedient. They had not refused to eat what they were told to but had done the opposite. They had eaten the fruit which God had told them not to. They knew the Lord would soon come and find them in the Garden of Eden and when they heard his voice in the cool of the day they were so frightened and ashamed that they tried to hide from

him. Where could they hope to hide from God? God is present everywhere and there is no place where his knowledge doesn't reach, but even so Adam and Eve pressed themselves into the shadows of the trees hoping that somehow they would be concealed. Of course they were soon found and punished for their disobedience. Death came into the world through their sin and they were banished from that glorious place, and prevented from ever coming back into it again.

But that was not the end of the story. The beauty of the Christian gospel is that it doesn't finish with disobedience and punishment. In spite of the sinfulness of our first parents, God in his love and mercy made a way by which we can once again be accepted as righteous in his sight and our disobedience forgiven.

In the New Testament we learn how Jesus came into this world, a 'second Adam', to suffer and to die in the place of those who trust in him, and to reveal the loving kindness of God.

The following text tells us how great God's love is. Think about it and pray over it. 'God so loved the world, that he gave his only begotten Son, that whosoever believeth in him should not perish, but have everlasting life' (John 3:16).

As a little girl I was disobedient, I was afraid, I hid but was found and scolded. Only later did I discover in the long lost letters how much Granny really loved me. In a very much greater way children must learn that if they disobey God's commands they too deserve punishment. But there is another great lesson. God has given a message in the Bible, letters and words, which tell not only of his commands but also of his love and care. Children, like adults, need to read that Word and

War Child

put their trust in Jesus. Only then will they understand how very great God's love is for them.

Bible Reading
Read Psalm 139 verses 1-12
to learn more about God's 'omnipresence'

Home and Away

The doorstep was smooth, worn thin by the feet of the family who had lived there for nearly forty years. All around were rough pebble stones taken up from the sea shore and regularly disturbed by the hens who scratched and pecked between them. But the stones had another use.

I used to love to sit in the sun on the step after lunch, with a plate of prunes. Once I had eaten the fruit all that was left were the stones. So I would pick up the large hard pebbles to crack open the prune stones in order to chew on the pips inside. They tasted rather bitter but it was a fun thing to do, particularly when my older cousin Andrew joined me on the doorstep and we counted out the pips between us.

At that stage I was still young and not old enough to go to school. I was also living on a Scottish island seven hundred miles away from my parents and with very little contact with them at all. They hadn't forgotten me however, and they wished all the time that we could be together. But I, and thousands of other children like me, had been 'evacuated' because of the war. We had all been sent off on trains from the big cities like London to keep us safe. Many of the children who were evacuated were sent away to live with strangers until the war ended.

I was 'evacuated' to four different places in all, but I ended up with my Granny and Aunty so I wasn't unhappy.

I enjoyed my time on the island even though there were no toys, books or television. There were other more exciting things than these to take up my time. The best of all were the hens. The 'chookies' were my special friends and I soon discovered they had secret nests that they would use instead of the hen house provided.

Whenever I heard a hen clucking I knew an egg had been laid. So I would go off hunting for it in the bracken.

When found I would gather the warm egg and carry it carefully into the kitchen to be cooked for tea.

My other favourite thing was 'Dandy' the dog who followed me wherever I went. He would have to be shut outside for the evening worship as he insisted on howling when the Psalm was sung.

Sometimes I went down to the shore to gather shellfish or to play in the rock pools. I loved to make imaginary houses in the rocks near to the school house where we lived. Once the school children had all gone home, I could get into one of the two classrooms and play with the chalk on the blackboard as if I was already in school.

In many ways it was a happy summer. No toys but plenty of freedom; no ice creams but plenty of eggs, rice pudding and prunes (though I hated the porridge!).

The important love and care came from Granny and Aunty, yet there was one thing missing. Home was where my parents were and I was away from them and I missed being with them so much. Then one day there was a wonderful surprise!

I was upstairs looking out of the window when I saw my mother and father opening the long metal gate at the end of the schoolhouse road. My whole family were going to be evacuated together to another place to get away from the bombs in London.

I didn't choose to be away from home. I didn't choose to leave my parents. Right from the beginning I wanted to be at home. However, in the Bible Jesus told a story about a boy who chose to be many miles away from his home

and family. It's called the 'Parable of the Lost Son' or the 'Prodigal Son'. ('Prodigal' means extravagant or wasteful and you can read the parable for yourself in Luke 15:11-32).

The first difference was that the 'Lost Son' did not need to be away from his father. I didn't choose to be on the Island but the son in Jesus' story chose to go away. He became tired of staying at home. He wanted to be free from the control of his parents and had convinced himself that he would be much happier away from home as he would be able to do whatever he wanted. The Bible says that he gathered together all he had and went off to a 'distant country'.

The son left the safety of his home to live in a place which was very dangerous for him. It was dangerous not

because there was a war on, or that there were bombs falling, but because he got into bad company. Far away from the guidance and security of his family, he began to enjoy himself, as he thought. He sinned more and more, and used up all his money until he had none left. He was poor, hungry and had to take the worst kind of work for a Jewish boy, working among the pigs, an unclean animal. He was so hungry that he would have gladly eaten the hard husks that the pigs were given.

But my story and the story of the Lost Son ended the same way. When my father came back to get me and to bring the family together again there was happiness, celebration and joy.

We had a very special treat when my parents arrived. A boiled chicken was served for tea. It was probably one of my hen friends who ended up as the welcome meal but I didn't mind. My family was together again.

The Bible tells us how the family of the Lost Son had a feast. A special calf that had been kept for an important occasion was killed for their celebration meal. The father said that the reason for the feast was that 'This my son was dead, and is alive again; he was lost, and is found.' He had come home after being far away and his loving father was overjoyed to have him back.

Home is to be with those we love and there is an empty feeling when we are away from them. But the story of

the Lost Son is about much more than being away and coming home. It teaches us about God the Father's love and willingness to receive us when we turn back to him in repentance and trust. Then we are brought into God's own family and at life's end we shall be taken to our eternal home, never to be separated from our heavenly Father again.

Bible Reading
Read about the Lost Son in
Luke 15:11-32

A Strong Dutch Tulip

I t was late November 1946 when Dora stepped off the boat train, which had come from Holland via Harwich. She disembarked onto a noisy, bleak platform at a station called Liverpool Street in London.

She was a teenager, all alone, and had come from a country still devastated by war. During the winter of 1944-45 there had been little food, no electricity or gas and no schooling because of the cold. Hungry people travelled from Amsterdam and The Hague to the small coastal town where Dora lived in order to buy very unusual 'vegetables' — tulip bulbs. Her father was a bulb grower who had barns full of tulips which he had been unable to export. There was little else left to eat so he sold them to the city dwellers for food.

At last the north of Holland was liberated, freed from German occupation and Dora's family began to rebuild their lives again.

One way was to get a visa to work in Britain, to learn English and benefit from the better food and conditions there at the time. So Dora left her home among the bulb fields and went to help in a Christian family in London for a year. This family happened to be our family and as I was just a few years younger than Dora the two of us began a strong friendship, which still continues after sixty years.

Dora went to English classes and became a fluent speaker and then returned to Holland to her father's home and the bulb fields. But not all the bulbs had been sold to the hungry city folk. Dora's father had secretly developed some new strains of tulip and hidden them in a glasshouse unknown even to the family. He decided to call each one by a different girl's name.

One particular tulip bulb sold extremely well. It was a late, tall, pure white flower. But what would they call it?

'What was the name of that girl in London? The one whose family you stayed with?' Dora's father asked her one day.

'Maurine,' she replied.

And that was how the bulb was named.

About forty years later, the real Maurine visited Holland and I was surprised to find several displays of my tulip in the bulb gardens at the Keukenhof. An article in a bulb grower's magazine commemorated my visit and it is still possible to buy that tulip in the U.K. after almost sixty years.

Most people think of Holland as the home of the flowering tulip bulb. But there is another association between the tulip and Holland. A very special tulip was produced by a large group of men. Thirty-three of them came from nine foreign countries outside Holland and spent six months meeting together working on a very important 'tulip'. It took one hundred and fifty-four meetings and a lot of hard work before this particular strong and resilient tulip came into being.

All this effort took place, not in the northern coastal bulb growing area of Holland, but in the oldest town of Holland nearer the south west of the country. At that time, during the winter of 1618-19, the town of Dordrecht was a well-known port.

The men meeting there did not dig the soil, nor did they plant seeds or bulbs. They spent their time studying the Bible and disputing with their opponents. Those six months were the time of a very famous church assembly. It was arranged by the Dutch Reformed Church to settle a serious theological controversy following the spread of 'Arminianism'.

After much hard work decisions were reached which were named after the town where the men were meeting. In the everyday English of the seventeenth century, Dordrecht was called 'Dort' and so the conclusions of the meetings became known as the Canons Of Dort. These statements (or judgements) set forth Reformed doctrine on points of difference from the Arminians.

The Arminian delegates raised five major points of difference and the Reformed Churches' responses to these have come to be referred to as the Five Points of Calvinism.

What have these got to do with a strong Dutch tulip? How was it possible to make a tulip out of a long conference of discussion, prayer and Bible study?

Well let me explain… this tulip is not a flower but a word, which helps us to remember that God is able to save all upon whom he has mercy. His efforts are not frustrated by the unrighteousness or the inability of humans.

The Five Points of Calvinism are these; Total depravity, Unconditional election, Limited atonement, Irresistible grace and the Perseverance of the saints. If you circle the capital letters of the five points, you will see that they make the word TULIP and that helps us to remember the words they stand for.

The Canons Of Dort still stand as part of the doctrinal foundations of Reformed churches. You may find them hard to understand but they are all part of God's plan of salvation and are anchors for our faith.

The white tulip produced in 1948 is still strong and vigorous. But the TULIP arrived at from

God's Word by the good men in Dordrecht in 1619 is much more important.

Perhaps now, when you see a tulip in bloom you will be reminded of the sovereign, eternal love and faithfulness of God towards his people.

Bible Reading
Look up John 10:27-28 and Philippians 1:6, texts which support the last of the points (Perseverance of the saints).

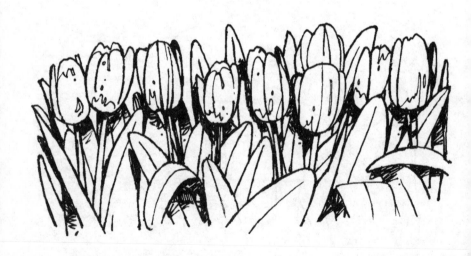

Flames in the Fog

This morning I pulled at the window blind and peered out into the dark winter skies. The garden was shrouded in a fine, white mist and I could see very little outside. As the sun came up the fog lifted and later in the day the mountain tops appeared. Beneath them, wispy bands of mist, contrasted with dark green pines and warm birches, still golden with a scattering of leaves. It was so beautiful, just like a delicate Chinese painting. Yet it reminded me of a different fog, dangerous and dirty, which over five dark days had killed four thousand city dwellers more than fifty years ago.

It was December 7th, 1952. I had been to church in central London with my parents and a Dutch friend, Corrie.

Corrie and I stayed on for lunch as there was always a meal on Communion Sunday since many folk travelled long distances to come to church. My parents decided to go home. Someone else would be able to give us a lift home. As it turned out, when evening came and darkness fell we couldn't find anyone to give us a lift.

And so it was that Corrie and I found ourselves with no option but to walk the whole five miles home. Perhaps that wasn't so bad – but that weekend was going to be different and would go down in London history for being a weekend of death.

The city didn't suffer from a dramatic hurricane, nor a disastrous tsunami, nor a blizzard or a flood, but it was SMOG — a deadly mixture of poisonous soot, sulphur and thick fog. It blocked out almost everything in sight, it smelt of rotten eggs and blackened even the blankets in the cupboard at home. People went out on the street with clean clothes only to return with them covered in soot.

As we walked I held my scarf up to cover my mouth and tried not to breathe the horrible mixture. It was dark, freezing cold and frightening. At first Corrie and I thought we could find our way home but then we realised that we couldn't even see the pavement. Few vehicles had ventured out as it was too dangerous to try to drive in such blackness. The only thing to do was to feel for the kerbs of the pavements and creep along in the right direction. It felt very scary and was very slow.

Then, out of the gloom we saw a large shape coming towards us, lit up inside but silhouetted against a huge fiery light. It was a London bus crawling along the kerbside very slowly. In front of it walked the bus conductor carrying a huge flaming flare. He held it high so the driver could follow it safely. Other buses appeared out of the gloom and soon we saw a number 3. 'We'll follow that one,' I exclaimed. 'It will take us in the right direction for some of the way.'

However once beyond the bus route we were totally lost. I knew that we were only a few streets from home but we couldn't see anything familiar to guide us on our way. No doubt my parents were praying that we would be brought safely home, and I too prayed for direction. After some moments of panic we finally found our bearings and eventually arrived back with our clothes and faces filthy, covered by the black sticky drops.

Life can be like that dangerous walk I had in the London Smog. The atmosphere around us can be evil, confusing and misleading. Indeed for many life is very frightening when they have nothing to guide them and they have no idea where they are going. There are lots of choices to make as we grow up and we need to learn how to avoid evil and sin.

Corrie and I were so thankful for the bus flares to keep us from straying. Each one of us also needs a clear light to guide us though the confusion of this world. The Old Testament (Exodus 13:21-22) tells how God led the Israelites through the desert in a very special way.

In the daytime a pillar of cloud overshadowed the huge encampment and by night it was revealed as a pillar of fire. It led the way in that wilderness where there were no tracks, roads or maps to follow, and it spoke to the Israelites of the presence of the Lord with them till they reached the Promised Land. That overhead fire must have felt something like the flares that I followed through the gloom of the smog, lightening the night and making the darkness less frightening.

Nowadays we do not usually have a flaming torch to lead us in our lives. Yet the Christian has an even clearer light to guide. God's Word gives general directives and some very specific ones to light up our paths. One of the clearest sets of directions are the Ten Commandments

(Exodus 20:1-17) but there are others right through the Bible so it is most important that we read God's Word regularly.

When I lost the light of the bus flare I had no idea which way to turn. So often when we lose our way it is because we are no longer following the light given to us in God's Word. The Psalmist understood this well when he wrote in Psalm 119 verse 105, 'Thy word is a lamp unto my feet, and a light unto my path'.

Bible Reading
Read Proverbs 3:5-6 to find out about who should be your guide in life.

Crowds for a Coronation

It was late in the evening and normally I would have been in bed. But today, June 1st 1953, was different. I was going to spend a night with two friends on a pavement in the centre of London.

I waved goodbye to my father who had taken us to Piccadilly Circus and my friends and I walked up the tree-lined Mall which stretches up to Buckingham Palace where the royal family live.

It was 11 p.m. but more and more people were gathering, determined to find a good spot where they would be able to see all that was going to happen the next day.

However, my friends and I couldn't find a good space in the Mall so had to walk on until we found a place that we could camp on the kerbside of St James' Street in front of some iron railings. These would be handy to climb up on the next day when we wanted a better view.

What was going to happen the next day? Well on June 2nd, the young Queen Elizabeth was to be crowned. Even though we weren't at the best spot on the mall the procession would go more slowly up the incline of St James' Street so we knew that we would be able to see the Queen in the gold coach with white horses as they passed.

We spent some time getting ourselves comfortable on the hard London pavement. We spread out our tartan rug and then opened our bag full of corned beef sandwiches wrapped in greaseproof paper. We also had some orange squash to drink. With our school Mackintosh coats and umbrellas we were ready for anything. There were no ipods, mobile phones or CDs to listen to in the 1950s but there was plenty to interest us. Street vendors came by, selling route maps of the procession and keepsake ornaments. The Cockney crowd was friendly and chatty,

and as dawn came up there was a buzz of excitement. The newspaper placards announced that the British expedition had reached the top of Mount Everest. They were the first men ever to climb it and just in time for the coronation. At long last, as the day wore on, we could hear the crowd roaring in the distance. The noise got neaier and nearer. It could only mean that the Queen was coming.

Everyone started to wave their flags and shout 'Hooray, long live the Queen!' and then it was over. The rain was pouring down. We huddled under the umbrellas and tried to spot which royal celebrities were in the other coaches.

A window behind us was thrown open and the diners inside offered us strawberries and cream to cheer us up. An open carriage drove by with the big, jolly Queen of Tonga standing up, ignoring the downpour and enjoying the huge welcome from the crowd.

By the evening, stiff, wet and exhausted, clutching half a bag of uneaten sandwiches, my friends and I joined the hundreds of weary Londoners walking to the bus stops and tube stations on their way home. It had been a day and night to remember, an adventure for teenagers, a taste of history.

In the Old Testament there are many stories about coronations and the crowds who watched them. My favourite when I was small was very different to the coronation in 1953. One difference was that the person

to be crowned was not a grown-up young lady but a little boy aged seven who was destined to be the king of Judah. He was called prince Joash and the first seven years of life must have been very hard for him.

He wasn't brought up in a rich palace where he could run around and play freely. He had to hide away in case he was discovered and killed.

Joash was a very special little boy. His parents were dead and all the other royal children had been murdered by Joash's evil grandmother Athaliah, daughter of the wicked King Ahab. Joash was the only one who had been saved. He had been rescued as a baby by his aunt and hidden in the temple by her husband Jehoida, the High Priest.

Athaliah now ruled the land of Judah but never went to worship in the beautiful temple of the Lord which stood so near to her palace. She was heathen and worshipped idols.

Another difference between the two coronations was that Joash's special day had to be kept a total secret in case the wicked Queen found out. So there were no crowds lining the streets, no holiday for the people, no big colourful ceremony. There was only a little lad standing beside a pillar of the temple where he could be seen clearly, waiting to be crowned.

The temple was crowded but the people there had a risky job to do. They were trusted men called from the different parts of the kingdom of Judah, armed with

swords and spears and told to stand guard and protect the young king from the followers of the Queen. No doubt they were delighted to discover that one of famous King David's descendants had been rescued and hidden. The high priest and his sons anointed the lad with oil, placed the crown on his head and everyone shouted 'God save the king' and clapped their hands with joy.

The coronation of Joash was a very important occasion in the history of God's people, the Jews. For many years, as long as his uncle the high priest was alive, Joash acted wisely and ruled in obedience to God's laws. Josah was also the only boy left of King David's royal line from which the Messiah had been promised. Many centuries later Jesus would be born and among his ancestors was King Joash, the little boy king. It is good for us to understand that God keeps his promises and is at work all through history. Sometimes when we cannot immediately see a reason for all the evil things happening in the world it is good to remember how one little boy was saved and hidden as part of God's overall plan.

Bible Reading
Read all about Joash in
2 Kings chapters 11 and 12, and in
2 Chronicles chapters 23 and 24.

My Name is Anne

During the second world war, like many British children I had to move around from place to place and spent the first two years of my school days in four different schools. Yet for many children elsewhere in Europe school life was even more difficult. One of these girls was called Jacquie.

Jacquie lived in Holland. She was really half French but her mother had a fashion business in Amsterdam and so the family settled there and enjoyed a comfortable life before the war. Her father was Jewish so the children became part of the wealthy Jewish community. Many of these families had become rich through the diamond trade based in the city.

Jacquie's family lived in a large comfortable home, attended good local schools and their friends were from families who went to one of the six synagogues in the city. Jacquie had lots of friends, lots of fun and a very good education. In spite of hearing the grown-ups speaking quietly as they worried about what was happening to Jews in nearby Germany, she had no idea of the danger

and welcomed the Jewish children who had fled from Germany to the apparent safety of Holland.

All this was to change once the Germans occupied Holland. No longer were Jewish families safe and the Nazi policy of Jewish persecution was about to begin in Amsterdam. Soon even the children were affected. Shortly before the start of the summer holidays the Jewish children who went to the same school as Jacquie were called into the headmaster's office and told that the school was no longer allowed to accept Jewish children.

As they left, boys called after them 'Jews, Jews' and they had to start the next term in a 'Jews only' school. That was only the beginning of the sadness. Jacquie had a best friend whom she had known for six years but a new regulation stated that Jewish children could no longer play in the homes of non-Jews. Jacquie could no longer visit her friend. No longer could she go to the local swimming pool, no longer could she sit on a public park bench or wander into any shop forbidden to the Jews. More and more the Jewish families suffered hatred and poverty.

Then, one day something happened to brighten up her life. A girl of around her own age came over to her and said, 'My name is Anne, Anne Frank.' Anne had come from Frankfurt in Germany and attended the Jewish School. The two girls became very close friends, constantly meeting and writing notes to each other. Life wasn't easy for the young teenagers. They were forced to wear a yellow star to show they were Jewish and Anne wrote, 'I don't dare do a thing any more because I'm afraid it isn't allowed.'

But worse was to come. Just after her 13th birthday Anne disappeared with no word to her friend. In fact she had gone into hiding and Jacquie was never to see her

again. In August 1944 the Germans discovered Anne's hiding place. Her family were sent to a concentration camp and she died from typhus in March 1945. Anne was to become very famous because of the diary she wrote during her two years in hiding. Jacquie survived the war and later wrote about her friendship with the girl who had become so famous.

It's easy to forget that the Jews were God's chosen people and that one day, in spite of all the hatred and persecution they have suffered over the centuries, they will be brought back into God's kingdom and will recognise that Jesus is their Messiah. But not only Jews suffer persecution. From the early days of the church

it was common for Christians to be persecuted and the book of Acts tells us how many suffered for their faith.

For some it was actually from the religious leaders that the hatred came. God used that hatred to scatter believers and so the gospel was spread around the Roman world and many new congregations of Christians came into being.

Later on, the persecution came from the people in power. Many believers were martyred in the big arena, the Coliseum, in Rome because they refused to worship the Roman Emperor. All through the ages there have been times when true believers have suffered for their faith. They have had to leave their homelands, been imprisoned or killed. It is not always easy to be a Christian and in many parts of the world nowadays even children are persecuted.

But if you trust in Jesus you can be sure that he will strengthen and uphold you whatever happens. Indeed Jesus himself taught his disciples that instead of persecution causing them to be sad they needed to see it in a totally different way. He told them that they were 'blessed' or 'happy' if persecution for 'righteousness' came their way. They were in fact to 'rejoice' because that suffering would bring its own reward when they reached heaven (Matthew 5:10-12).

Bible Reading
Read the book of Acts and you will see how suffering in itself was used by God to spread the Gospel Truth.

The Hiding Place

It was summer 1951, just six years after the end of World War Two. It was my family's first visit to Holland. We had arrived very late at night, thankful to reach the home of Christian friends after a long drive through dark and fog. The little house was warm and welcoming, set in a small town in the centre of the country. It seemed very normal and attractive, with a traditional red tiled pointed roof, attic style bedrooms and enclosed garden, which even had a traditional well next to a walnut tree. Yet it was only a few years since the family living there, two teenage boys and a girl with their parents, had gone through a dangerous and difficult time when the Germans occupied Holland.

One problem was that any boys or young men were rounded up and sent off to work in Eastern Europe doing hard labour in armament factories. Families feared the German Military who regularly hunted their homes for teenage boys. Some boys lived in cellars and only came out at night. Others hid when there was a warning signal. And so the innocent looking little house had its own secrets and all was not what it seemed to be.

Three parts of the home were misleading. First, if visitors stood outside in the garden and looked up to the roof, all they could see were rows of curved brick coloured tiles, slotting closely into each other. But someone who knew the secret could climb up on to the roof, lift a group of loose tiles and crawl through the hole into the loft until danger was past.

Nearby stood the well, looking just like an illustration for the nursery rhyme 'Jack and Jill'. It too had a red tiled roof, and a noisy chain with a metal bucket hooked on to it. Once again, things weren't as they seemed. There was no water in this well and it only pretended to sink deep down into the earth. It was there to confuse and make a noise!

Back inside the home there was another false trail. On the wall of the spare bedroom was a large recess, set up like a small shrine, or worship centre, with candles and a prayer book.

The family were not Roman Catholics and the shrine was a fake concealing another small opening, through which the boys could escape into the loft at the first hint of danger.

So the pattern was something like this. Warning would come that the German military were in the street looking for boys. As quickly as possible the boys would crawl through the bedroom wall and hide till the search was over.

It was hoped that the soldiers would not want to disturb a religious shrine and would not find the loft space. And they never did. But what if one of the boys was outside and had no time to get indoors before the soldiers went in? Then the escape had to be through the tiled roof and here it was that the well came into use.

The mother of the family could start to turn the wheel and draw up the bucket with the clanking metal chain, hoping that no-one would hear the noise of the roof tiles being moved and put back into place.

Once again, the plan worked and by God's grace, the boys survived the war at home and were never caught. When the country was freed, many other young men came out into the open from the cellars with chalk white faces because they had seen no daylight for up to two years.

What has the story of a secret hiding place for two young Dutchmen over fifty years ago got to do with young people today? It has to do with the ideas which lay behind many of the causes of that terrible war which destroyed fifty million people in less than six years as well as six million Jews and others in the German concentration camps.

The Bible says, speaking about man, 'As he thinketh in his heart, so is he' (Proverbs 23:7).

For each one of us the beliefs and standards we hold dear influence how we live our individual lives. The same principle works out in nations and the rulers over them. Very often wars may be about fighting for scarce resources like land and water, but more often during the centuries, wars have been because leaders have sought power and control over the countries around them. But the Second World War had a more sinister wickedness behind it.

Adolf Hitler, the Leader of Germany, held ideas rooted in evolutionary thought and used those ideas to justify his aggression and mass murder. He believed in the 'survival of the fittest' and so was prepared to get rid of those who were mentally sick or physically handicapped. He had no mercy for the weak in society and indeed believed that the 'pure' Teutonic Germans were a 'master race' who had a right to conquer the world.

He believed in evolution and not the special creation of mankind and thus people were easily expendable as merely part of a development from early forms of life. His compelling personality led many Germans to believe these ideas and to support him to the very end of a war that tore Europe apart.

These ideas came from a book written by an Englishman, Charles Darwin. It is very famous and was

entitled 'On the Origin of Species by means of Natural Selection,' subtitled 'The Preservation of Favoured Races in the Struggle for Life.'

Not only Hitler, but the Communist leaders Stalin (in U.S.S.R.), Mao (in China) and Pol Pot (in Cambodia) used this wicked, atheistic principle of the 'survival of the fittest' to destroy millions of innocent people during the 20th century. For Stalin, Mao and Pol Pot it was a class struggle and for Hitler it was a racial struggle. These men are among the world's worst mass murderers.

Such thinking is far removed from what the Bible teaches. Genesis tells us that man was created in God's image and so every person is to be respected as human and not to be treated according to race, abilities and strength. The expression of the Christian faith is one of love and care to those who need it, not destruction and cruelty. It seems impossible that such cruelty should have taken hold in Germany, a country that was the cradle of the Reformation under Martin Luther but it serves as a warning to us today.

The atheistic ideas of evolution are still being taught in our schools and constantly repeated in T.V. programmes as if they were facts. We must be aware not just of the falsity of these theories but also of the way they may influence what happens in our land. Although sadly, many abortions happen, yet it is a belief in what Christians call 'the sanctity of life' that still stops our society killing off unwanted babies, the mentally ill, old folk and long term sick. Thankfully Hitler did not ultimately succeed in his plans to conquer Britain and some Christian values still underpin our society.

If you are being taught evolution as fact remember how damaging such ideas can turn out to be. Hold fast to the Biblical account of creation and know that you as well as all others have a special place in God's creation, made in the image of God.

Bible Reading
Read Psalm 14:1 to find out what God says about atheists.

Who is Maurine Murchison?

Maurine Murchison was born in London but when war broke out she was moved, for her own safety, to the island of Rasaay to live with her grandmother. The bombing raids on London, later to be called The Blitz, meant that many families were separated from each other during the war years. Government regulations were such that thousands of children were evacuated from the towns and cities at that time. Maurine's family were no exception. However, they were eventually reunited when her father Dr. Murdoch Tallach took a war time post in Law Hospital in Carluke, Scotland. At the age of thirteen she professed her faith in Jesus Christ as her Lord and Saviour. This faith and this Saviour would never leave her.

After school Maurine went to Edinburgh University where she excelled at History. It was there that she met her future husband, who was also named Murdoch and was also a doctor. Her graduation day was also the day she got engaged. In 1959 Maurine and Murdoch were married in Westminster Chapel, London. They lived initially in London and Peru, moving to Inverness in 1964.

It was there that Maurine began a project that she would later describe as one of the most important projects of her life.

Alongside her growing family Maurine was responsible for the formation of a new group of Bible studies. Initially based at her home in Island Bank Road – these new women's Bible studies soon blossomed and after only a few years amounted to almost 500 different groups.

Amongst other things she was influential in the early development of the Children's Panel in the Highlands of Scotland as well as being involved in other local and national government committees. In 1984 she was awarded the O.B.E.

Maurine and her husband lived in Aberdeen for some ten years before settling back in the old family home in Strathpeffer in 1995.

After collapsing on holiday while in Egypt, Maurine was discovered to have a heart condition, but one that could be operated on successfully. However, on 17th April, 2008 after she was operated on at the Royal Sussex County Hospital in Brighton, she never fully regained consciousness and died peacefully, trusting in Jesus, on 19th April.

Her husband and family have fond memories of her and are grateful to God for her example and consistent witness. They remember Maurine as a woman of strong Christian influence in her family and also in the roles that she played at a local and national level.

Psalms for Life

The following verses were sung at Maurine's funeral. When you read them think about how helpful they are. You can take them anywhere – into the Blitz, on an evacuation train, throughout your whole life.

Psalm 103: 1–4

O thou my soul, bless God the Lord;
and all that in me is
Be stirred up his holy name
to magnify and bless.

Bless, O my soul, the Lord thy God,
and not forgetful be
Of all his gracious benefits
he hath bestowed on thee.

All thine iniquities who doth
most graciously forgive:
Who thy diseases all and pains
doth heal, and thee relieve.

Who doth redeem thy life, that thou
to death may'st not go down;
Who thee with loving-kindness doth
And tender mercies crown.

Psalm 71: 14–17

But I with expectation
will hope continually;
And yet with praises more and more
I will thee magnify.

Thy justice and salvation
my mouth abroad shall show,
Ev'n all the day; for I thereof
the numbers do not know.

And I will constantly go on
in strength of God the Lord;
And thine own righteousness, ev'n thine
alone, I will record.

For even from my youth, O God,
by thee I have been taught;
And hitherto I have declared
the wonders thou hast wrought.

Psalm 73: 23–26

Nevertheless continually
O Lord, I am with thee:
Thou dost me hold by my right hand,
and still upholdest me.

Thou, with thy counsel, while I live,
wilt me conduct and guide;
And to thy glory afterward
receive me to abide.

Whom have I in the heavens high
but thee, O Lord, alone?
And in the earth whom I desire
besides thee there is none.

My flesh and heart doth faint and fail,
but God doth fail me never:
For of my heart God is the strength
and portion for ever.

What was the Second World War?

From 1939 until 1945 the United Kingdom fought alongside its allies. It was one of the most terrible wars that country had ever been involved in. It was a total war – which means that every person and business in the contributing countries were involved in some way.

Sixty-one different nations fought in World War II. These countries had a total of 1.7 billion citizens, which meant that three quarters of the entire world's population were involved. Fifty million people were killed during the fighting and many millions were injured.

But how did this war actually start? Well it all started with another War – World War I. Germany had lost that war and as a result had to give up land that had once belonged to it. Germany was also banned from having an army of its own. But in 1933 Germany voted in a new leader named Adolf Hitler. He led a political party called the National Socialists or Nazis. Hitler made promises to the Germans. He was going to make Germany a great nation once again so he immediately began to re-arm the country and to seize land from other places like Czechoslovakia.

On the 1st of September 1939 Germany invaded the country of Poland. Because Britain and France had already signed a treaty with Poland to protect it in case of attack – the Prime Minister of Britain, Neville Chamberlain, declared war on Germany. Chamberlain realised that a National Government of all political parties was necessary during this time of conflict. Chamberlain resigned and was replaced by Winston Churchill.

Who was Who in the Second World War?

There were several leaders involved in the Second World war. Some were attackers and others were defenders.

Adolf Hitler was the dictator of Germany (1933-45) and started World War II. He divided mankind into racial groupings with Germans (or Aryans) at the top. Other races were ranked as less important and Jewish people were not even considered to be human. Germans, as the Master race were to take over the world and eliminate the Jews. The reality was that Hitler lost the war, his country was defeated and he took his own life. The leaders of those nations who stood against Nazi Germany are still remembered to this day.

Winston Churchill had long warned of the danger of Nazi Germany. However, the United Kingdom under Prime Minister Neville Chamberlain wanted peace at all costs. Chamberlain's government collapsed when this policy did not succeed. Churchill became prime minister on May 10, 1940 on the same day that Germany invaded France. France was soon defeated and the United Kingdom came under threat itself from air and sea. Germany's airforce bombed cities and ports. Their ships and submarines attacked the navy and merchant shipping. Churchill however was the ideal wartime leader. He kept up the national morale and today he is remembered as one of the most prominent national leaders in history.

Josef Stalin was a brutal Communist dictator of Russia (1928-1953). He was responsible for the death of millions of Russian citizens prior to the Second World War. In 1939 he made an alliance with Hitler in order to protect Russia. As part of the deal Russia invaded Poland at the same time as Germany thus starting World War II. However in 1941 Hitler broke this treaty and invaded Russia. The Russian military finally succeeded against the Nazi forces but after the war was over Stalin's brutal regime continued until his death in 1953.

Franklin D Roosevelt, was president of the United States of America (1933-1945). He realized that Adolf Hitler was a global threat and persuaded Congress to allow the United States to sell weapons to Britain and France and eventually Russia. When Japan issued a surprise attack on the US naval and air bases in Pearl Harbour, Hawaii, on 7th December, 1941 the US joined the war alongside Britain and Russia. Roosevelt died in April 1945, shortly before the end of the war, and was succeeded by vice president Harry S. Truman.

Charles de Gaulle assumed command of the newly-created French 4th Mechanized Division in May 1940, just as the German invasion began. He did not save his country, but was appointed Under-Secretary for War and was in London when France fell. The government of which de Gaulle was a member refused to surrender. However, this government was replaced by one led by Marshal Petain who did surrender. De Gaulle refused to accept this new government, and made a radio broadcast to the French people, saying - 'France has lost a battle, she has not lost the war.'

TWO WELL-KNOWN CHRISTIANS FROM THE SECOND WORLD WAR

Corrie ten Boom lived in Holland during the second world war. She was a committed Christian and loved to look after handicapped children. Her father had prayed for many years for God's people, the Jews, so when Germany invaded Holland Corrie and other members of her family joined the Dutch Resistance. They hid Jewish people in a secret room in their house. But when they were discovered Corrie and her sister Betsie and their father Casper ten Boom were arrested. Corrie and Betsie were imprisoned in a concentration camp where Betsie eventually died. Corrie escaped when one of the Nazi staff made an administration error. After the war, Corrie spent a lot of her time writing and speaking about her time in the camp and how God looked after her and taught her to forgive her enemies.

Dietrich Bonhoeffer was a German pastor who belonged to the part of the German Church called the Confessing Church. They did not agree with the National Socialist Government. Some people tried to persuade Dietrich to leave Germany for the safety of the United States but he refused. Dietrich rather chose to stay in his country in order to support the resistance there. He was a double agent. While serving for German military intelligence he also served as a courier for the German resistance movement. He was eventually imprisoned in 1943. During his time in prison he ministered to his fellow inmates and the guards. When his involvement in the plot to kill Adolf Hitler was discovered he was transferred from a military prison to a detention cellar in the Gestapo's high security prison. Shortly before the war ended in 1945 Dietrich was executed. The camp Doctor who witnessed his execution said that he saw Bonhoeffer pray before he died. 'I have hardly ever seen a man die so entirely submissive to the will of God.'

Second World War Time Line

15th March 1939 – Hitler invades Czechoslovakia

21st March 1939 – Hitler demands the free city of Danzig

29th March 1939 – Britain and France pledge to support Poland

7th April 1939 – Italy invades Albania

23rd August 1939 – Stalin and Hitler sign the Nazi-Soviet pact

1st September 1939 – Germany invades Poland

3rd September 1939 – U.K. and France declare war on Germany

Churchill appointed as First Lord of the Admiralty

21st September 1939 – All Jews in Poland imprisoned in ghettos

27th September 1939 – Polish army surrenders

30th October 1939 – U.S. declares neutrality

30th November 1939 – Finland invaded by Russia

9th April 1940 – Germany invades Denmark and Norway

10th May 1940 – Germany invades France

Churchill replaces Chamberlain as Prime Minister of U.K.

14th May 1940 – Netherlands surrenders

27th May 1940 – Evacuation of allied troops at Dunkirk

14th June 1940 – German army enters Paris

22nd June 1940 – France signs treaty with Germany

28th June 1940 – Charles de Gaulle becomes leader of Free French

10th July 1940 – German airforce begins Battle of Britain

23rd August 1940 – The Blitz begins

25th August 1940 – R.A.F. bombs Berlin

27th September 1940 – Japan signs a treaty with Germany and Italy

17th April 1941 – Yugoslavia surrenders to Germany

21st April 1941 – Greece surrenders to Germany

10th May 1941 – German airforce destroys House of Commons

12th August 1941 – Germany advances on Leningrad

20th September 1941 – Germany captures Kiev

6th October 1941 – Germany advances on Moscow

7th December 1941 – Japan attacks the U.S. at Pearl Harbour in Hawaii

8th December 1941 – Japan invades Malaya, Thailand and Philippines

11th December 1941 - U.S. declares war on Germany

11th December 1941 – Japan invades Burma

8th February 1942 – Japan invades Singapore

18th April 1942 – U.S. bombs Tokyo

3rd June 1942 – Battle of Midway begins

4th November 1942 – German Army defeated at El Alamein

25th July 1943 – Mussolini removed from power in Italy

13th June 1944 – First V1 flying bomb used on U.K.

4th February 1945 – Churchill, Stalin and Roosevelt meet at the Yalta conference

22nd March 1945 – U.S. army crosses the Rhine

27th March 1945 – Last V2 Rocket lands on U.K.

30th April 1945 – Hitler commits suicide

4th May 1945 – All German military surrenders

8th May 1945 – Winston Churchill announces V.E. Day

6th/9th August 1945 – U.S. drops two atomic bombs on Japan

2nd September 1945 – Japan surrenders

Second World War Daily Life

There are many ways that life today is different from life during the second world war. People had to wear gas masks for fear of a German gas attack. You had to use special material to cover your windows at night. This was called The Black Out. Its purpose was to stop enemy planes from seeing the light from a window and aiming a bomb at it.

Children who lived in the big cities during the war were often evacuated to the safety of the country. And everyone in the U.K. at that time had to have ration books.

Let's find out a bit more about what evacuation was. One of the ways that the government protected the population during the war years was to evacuate children from the danger zones.

What does the word evacuation mean? It means to leave a place. Because the government was worried that British cities and towns would be targets for German bombing raids, children and some women were evacuated to the countryside. It was only a temporary measure and often once people felt that the danger had passed the children would return to their families only to be evacuated again once the fighting re-commenced.

The British evacuation began on Friday 1st September 1939. It was called 'Operation Pied Piper.' Why do you think it was called that?

Special Billeting officers were put in charge of finding homes for the evacuees. Householders in the country were paid money by the government for taking in children who were evacuated.

During the evacuation children had labels attached to them so that people would know who they were, where they were going to and whom they belonged. They would then be packed onto a train and taken to different places across the United Kingdom. On arrival at their destination they would often be taken to a village hall where host families would pick what child they wanted most. Often it was the better looking children that were chosen first. The sickly looking children would be left until last.

What about rationing though? During the Second World War the Nazi forces tried to stop supplies of food and other goods from getting into Britain. Before the war began the United Kingdom would import 55 million tons of food. A month after the war this figure dropped to 12 million. So it was necessary to make sure that everyone had their fair share of the food and other items that were hard to get hold of during the war.

On the 29th of September 1939 every householder had to fill in a form giving details of who lived in their house. Using that information the government issued everyone with an identity card and ration book. The books contained coupons that had to be handed to or signed by the shopkeeper every time rationed goods were purchased.

This meant that you could only buy the amount that you were allowed. These books didn't replace money – you still had to pay for your goods as normal.

The food stuffs that were rationed included meat; fish; cheese; rice; jam; tea; eggs; canned fruit; biscuits; breakfast cereals; milk; dried fruit and cooking fat.

A typical ration for one person per week was:
Butter 50g
Bacon and ham 100g
Margarine 100g
Sugar 225g
Milk 3 pints
Cheese 50g
1 fresh egg a week
Tea 50g
Jam 450g every two months
Sweets 350g every four weeks

In addition to that you were also allowed sixteen extra points per month to use on whatever food items you wished.

When we think about what people had to go through during the Second World War we should be thankful for the food that we have, for the times of peace and for our freeuom. Thank God for those people who were willing to put their lives at risk in order to protect your country. And be thankful for the many blessings that God has given you.

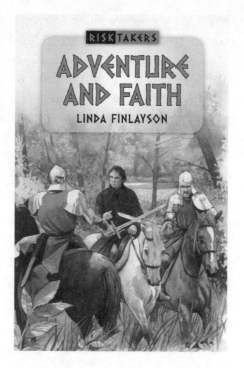

A NEW SERIES OF REAL LIFE ADVENTURES!

Adventure and Faith

by Linda Finlayson

ISBN: 978-1-84550-491-5

Martin Luther is accused of being a criminal but he has to stand up for what he believes. David Brainerd ventures into difficult wilderness territory in order to share the gospel. For William King it doesn't matter what the powerful slave owners want – Jesus has other plans. Brother Andrew risks his life so that Hungarians can read the Bible. But what about the Soviet troops who have invaded the country? Nehemiah builds a wall while enemies plot to destroy his work. Stephen prays to Jesus as an angry mob throws stones at him.

These men were all willing to take risks. While reading their exciting stories you will learn about why they did what they did and who it was that helped them.

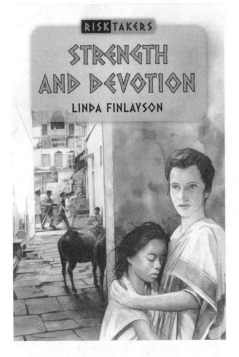

A NEW SERIES OF REAL LIFE ADVENTURES!

Strength and Devotion

by Linda Finlayson

ISBN: 978-1-84550-492-2

Katherine von Bora escapes to freedom in a fish- monger's cart – all because she must worship God as the Bible tells her to. Fidelia Fiske teaches Iranian children about Jesus but it brings danger to her door. Amy Carmichael helps a young Christian woman escape her angry family under cover of darkness. Lillian Dickson treks through hostile jungle in order to reach remote villages with the good news of Jesus Christ. Deborah takes charge of an army when no one else has the courage. Jehosheba risks her life to rescue her nephew. The throne of Israel and more is saved because of her actions.

These women were all willing to take risks. While reading their exciting stories you will learn about why they did what they did and who it was that helped them.

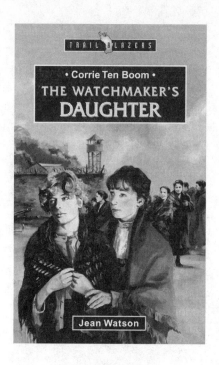

TRAILBLAZERS
A REAL WORLD WAR TWO ADVENTURE
The Watchmaker's Daughter
by Jean Watson

ISBN: 978-1-85792-116-8

The story of Corrie ten Boom has inspired millions of people all over the world. Jean Watson is a skilful author and presents Corrie's stirring life and challenging hope-filled message for young readers.

The Watchmaker's Daughter traces the life of this outstanding Christian woman from her childhood in Haarlem, through her suffering in Nazi concentration camps, to her world-wide ministry to the handicapped and underprivileged.

This exciting victorious book will allow you to meet this beloved woman and learn of God's wonderful provision and blessing through adversity.

TRAILBLAZERS
A REAL TWENTIETH CENTURY ADVENTURE
A Voice in the Dark
by Catherine Mackenzie
ISBN: 978-1-85792-298-1

Arrested by the Government of Romania in the 1960s, Richard
Wurmbrand was convicted of a crime - loving Jesus.

Catherine Mackenzie retells Richard's gripping, and at
times gruesome story. Despite suffering years of mental and
physical torture, God used Richard to witness to many people
from prison guards to government officials. Even after his
release from prison Richard prayed that if God could use him
to reach others for Christ, to send him back.

God heard his prayer and Richard was re-arrested and sent to
prison for another period of torture. His story is inspirational.

RESCUE
AND
REDEEM

Volume 5: Chronicles of the Modern Church

HISTORY LIVES

Mindy and Brandon Withrow

HISTORY LIVES
RESCUE AND REDEEM
VOLUME 5: CHRONICLES OF THE MODERN CHURCH
by Mindy and Brandon Withrow
ISBN: 978-1-84550-433-5

Let history come to life - just the way it should do. As the modern world exploded with rapid changes - in transportation, in communication, in manufacturing - people around the globe faced overwhelming new challenges. As Christians arrived for the first time in other countries, they realized that being a Christian was about living out the gospel in every culture. And they realized that great injustice was everywhere! So they met the challenges of modern life with new ways of communicating Christ's ancient gospel. From Niijima Jo and Pandita Ramabai to Dietrich Bonhoeffer and Janani Luwum, they set out to rescue God's global people and redeem them to new life in Christ.

Extra features throughout this book look deeper into issues such as modern Bible translation, living the Golden Rule, new developments in missions, and big moments in modern Christianity.

The fifth book in a series intended to cover the history of the Christian church through its people and key events. Written primarily for 9-14 year olds with a modern, relaxed and enthusiastic style. Many adults also enjoy these as a good read. This is history without the wooliness – and with all the wonder.